THE FIRESIGN THEATRE:

WAITING FOR THE ELECTRICIAN, OR SOMEONE LIKE HIM
&
TEMPORARILY HUMBOLDT COUNTY

Phil Austin, Peter Bergman,
David Ossman & Phil Proctor
stage adaptation by
David Ossman

BROADWAY PLAY PUBLISHING INC
224 E 62nd St, NY NY 10065-8201
212 772-8334 fax: 212 772-8358
BroadwayPlayPubl.com

First printing: December 2011
I S B N: 978-0-88145-510-6

Book design: Marie Donovan
Page make-up: Adobe Indesign
Typeface: Palatino
Printed and bound in the U S A

CONTENTS

ABOUT THE AUTHORS

The Firesign Theatre (Phil Austin, Peter Bergman, David Ossman, Phil Proctor) began working together as pioneers in radio improv and studio-produced audio "movies for your mind." Their unusual collaborative writing technique led to genre- and media-melding short plays, first introduced in rock and folk clubs around Los Angeles in 1967. These included takes on Sherlock Holmes (*Hemlock Stones*) and Republic cliff-hangers (*The Fuse of Doom*), the Faustian acid-trip, *Freek For A Week* and a musical vaudeville, *The American Pageant.*"

From Firesign's hit L Ps come the classics: immortal radio detective *Nick Danger,* surreal nightmare comedy *Waiting For The Electrician,* a sketch about how the West was won, *Temporarily Humboldt County,* and their most popular story, *Don't Crush That Dwarf, Hand Me The Pliers.*

For their 1974 Carnegie Hall performance and tour, Firesign adapted their four best-selling L Ps into a two-act play, *Anytown U S A*

Letting their theatrical imaginations have full reign, Firesign developed three very different performances over as many years, debuting them at a famous rock club, The Roxy. The finale, 1980s *Fighting Clowns* was an in-your-face Brechtian musical revue. In its 45th year, Firesign continues to present its work theatrically to its loyal following across America.

Since the 1970s, the group has answered many requests for performance rights to their recorded and published work. These newly published versions, which incorporate staging ideas based on years of Firesign's own performances, now will happily answer those requests.

Outside of The Firesign Theatre, its members have had a variety of professional careers in radio, film, theater, and television as writers, producers, actors and voice artists. More information about them and about Firesign's recorded and published work can be found at firesigntheatre.com and at the Firesign Theatre's Facebook site.

WAITING FOR THE ELECTRICIAN, OR SOMEONE LIKE HIM

Scene One—The Terminal

("P"—A nice-looking young person with a backpack—has just gotten off an airplane after a long flight. P makes his way off the ramp. This is not Paris or London. This is a crummy little airport, dingy and slightly frightening. P is listening on a pair of earphones. We hear what P's hearing over a pair of large speakers flanking the stage.)

SPEAKER VOICE: (Briskly) This is Side Five. Follow in your book and repeat after me as we learn three new words in Turkish...

P: Oh... O K... Right...

SPEAKER VOICE: Towel ....

P: (Repeats) Towel...

SPEAKER VOICE: Bath...

P: Ba-ath...

SPEAKER VOICE: Border...

P: Bor-der...

SPEAKER VOICE: May I see...

P: (Repeating) May I-ee see...

SPEAKER VOICE: ...your passport, please?

P: yo-ur pas-sport...

(The big speakers suddenly play airport music.)

(A border patrol GUARD armed with an automatic weapon stops P with one hand.)

BIG GUARD: Please! May I see your passport?

P: Well, sure... *(He shrugs off the backpack, sets it down and zips open a pocket.)*

P: I have it right here

(P pulls out his passport. The BIG GUARD flips it open, looks carefully back and forth at the picture and at P, then flips to the back of the passport where he discovers something suspicious. He rips the page out, tucks it in his pocket and calls out to another GUARD, who is lounging by the doorway.)

BIG GUARD: Hmmmmm... Look at this!

(The second GUARD, a shorter person, saunters over, takes the passport, examines it, tucks it in his pocket and snaps his fingers at the BIG GUARD who reluctantly hands over the page he ripped out. The SMALL GUARD looks at it, then at P.)

SMALL GUARD: Hmmmmm... This photograph doesn't look a bit like you, now does it sir? *(He tucks the picture away in his pocket.)*

P: Well...it was an old picture...

BOTH GUARDS: Precisely!

P: Is there anything wrong?

BIG GUARD: Oh, no, no, no, no...

SMALL GUARD: No, no, no, no!

(The BIG GUARD takes P's backpack and puts it "over the Border.")

BIG GUARD: Would you mind waiting over there.

(P reaches for the backpack, the BIG GUARD moves it further away.)

BIG GUARD: Over there, please!

P: But my passport!

(The SMALL GUARD *walks away with the passport in his pocket. The* BIG GUARD *gestures to the non-existent "line".)*

BIG GUARD: Next, please!

(Both GUARDS *stroll off to a corner where they examine the contents of P's backpack. Confused, but not discouraged, P looks around and spots a possibly helpful person. He wears a large badge that says "INFORMATION" and sports a mobile phone plugged into his ear. P approaches him and is about to ask a question when the* INFO MAN *speaks.)*

INFO MAN: *(He has a strong, but non-specific accent)* Information! May I help you?

P: Yes, thanks. I'd like to know...

INFO MAN: *(Listening to the phone, then:)* Not for twelve hours! You'll be informed at your hotel.

P: Yes, but...

INFO MAN: Would you like to send a wireless?

P: Yes, I guess I better...

INFO MAN: One moment, please...

(The INFO MAN *strolls over to look at the contents of P's backpack which the* GUARDS *are spreading out. P watches in frustration. A* WIRELESS OP *with a tablet computer taps him on the shoulder. She is very secretive.)*

WIRELESS OP: Do you want this Government Overnight, Standard Economy or Guaranteed Delivery?

P: Well, which is fastest?

(The WIRELESS OP *taps some code into the tablet, waits a moment for the information to appear, then:)*

WIRELESS OP: Hunh! At this time of day they all receive equal attention, depending of course *(pointedly)* on the Zone involved.

P: Zone? I'm sending it overseas.

WIRELESS OP: *(This is crucial)* No! Please! The Zone! Look at the map!

(The WIRELESS OP *shows him the tablet. P looks at the screen, trying to interpret the information. Meanwhile, the* GUARDS *have discovered some interesting evidence, which they discuss.)*

P: Oh, well, then, I suppose it would be...

(The BIG GUARD *comes sternly up to P and opens his palm to reveal a bar of soap.)*

BIG GUARD: I beg your pardon, sir, but is this your bar of soap?

(Taking in the situation, seeing his stuff spilled out on the table, P takes the wisest course:)

P: Well, sure, yes, I suppose it is...

(The GUARDS *exchange significant glances. The* INFO MAN *speaks a few words into his cell phone. The* SMALL GUARD *zips up P's backpack, tosses it to the* INFO MAN, *who carries it away.)*

BIG GUARD: So do we...

(Before P can protest, the WIRELESS OP *looks up from her tablet to report:)*

WIRELESS OP: All right, sir, your wireless has been sent. *(Aside, confidentially)* You'll be receiving it in about an hour, Guaranteed Delivery! *(Aloud)* That will be two-hundred-and-seventy-five, sir. No tax.

P: Gosh, I haven't had a chance to change my money yet...

(The SMALL GUARD *finds a child's Mickey Mouse backpack somewhere and shows it to the* BIG GUARD, *who calls out:)*

BIG GUARD: Just a moment, sir!

SMALL GUARD: Is this your bag?

P: *(This is a silly question)* No, it's not.

(The SMALL GUARD *brings the Mickey bag over to* P.)

SMALL GUARD: Check it again. Do take your time, sir.

P: That is definitely not my bag!

SMALL GUARD: *(Thoughtfully)* Just as we thought...

(As the SMALL GUARD *returns the bag to behind the Border, each of the other officials takes a clipboard with a ballpoint pen attached by a string and holds them out to* P.)

WIRELESS OP: Sign here, please.

(P does so. OP disappears discreetly, her mission accomplished.)

BIG GUARD: And here...

INFO MAN: And here...

SMALL GUARD: And here...

(The BIG GUARD *flips up a second page. This is the last one, we think.)*

BIG GUARD: And here.

(The BIG GUARD *walks away.* P *thinks it's over. But no, the* SMALL GUARD *has a second form to sign.)*

SMALL GUARD: And here!

INFO MAN: *(Listening to his phone, then)* We've sent your bag on ahead sir. Where is it that you're staying?

P: *(His expectations are not high)* Uh...what's the best hotel in town?

INFO MAN: *(Dubiously)* Of course! *(He steps out as if to hail a cab)* Taxi!

(The SMALL GUARD *looks at him as if to say, "you nuts?")*

INFO MAN: *(Apologetically)* Oh! Ha, ha ha! The taxis— they are all on strike.

SMALL GUARD: *(It's obvious)* And it's too early for the bus.

INFO MAN: *(Menacingly)* You really are a problem, sir.

SMALL GUARD: *(Resigned)* I suppose we'll have to put you up.

(An elevator door opens and the ELEVATOR "BOY" stands waiting. Elevator music.)

Scene Two: The Elevator

(Inside the elevator are two passengers—the FELLOW TRAVELER, who does all the talking—and the GUY with a newspaper, who hides his face behind the headlines and never speaks. The elevator "BOY" is also [almost] silent as he mimes the pulling of the door closed, starting the old-fashioned gears, stopping at each of the several floors with an audible "ding," opening the door, closing it and moving on up. [The "BOY" is played by the woman in the company.])

FELLOW TRAVELER: *Skajityeh tovarish! Kak vwee padoomityeh a nashyeh gorodyea?* ...Oh, excuse me, but my friend would like to know how much you have enjoyed our City so far?

P: Actually, I haven't been here too long.

FELLOW TRAVELER: *Il n'est pas passé beaucoup de temps ici... Noo! Rasskazivayetsah meenyagh "dah" elee "nyet!"*... Oh! He want to know"yes" or "no".

P: *(This is getting a little strange)* Well, tell him "yes." *(Raising his voice)* It's a beautiful city!

FELLOW TRAVELER: *Nyeh krichayehteh! Ya slichayoo!* ...He says, "He can shout, don't hear you.

"BOY": Ding!

("BOY" goes through her door open and close routine. The silent GUY turns the pages of his paper.)

FELLOW TRAVELER: Have you seen the Palace?

P: Not yet...

(Reacting to the FELLOW TRAVELER'*s severe look)*

P: But I certainly intend to.

FELLOW TRAVELER: Oh, you must, you must! It won't be here much longer, you know. *(This is a secret)* They are cleaning it!

"BOY": Ding!

*(Once again "*BOY*" opens and closes the door. P thinks maybe he should get out, but once he makes up his mind, it's too late, the door is shut and the elevator moving again. An uncomfortable pause.*

FELLOW TRAVELER: *On yedeenstvehnee?*...Are you alone?

P: *(This makes him really nervous)* ...Yes...

FELLOW TRAVELER: *Non!* We are here with you!

P: *(Not reassured)* Oh. I see what you mean. Uh, no...

FELLOW TRAVELER: Yes! ...How many are we?

P: Here? *(Looks around)* ...Three?

"BOY": Ding!

FELLOW TRAVELER: You don't want to count the Elevator Boy?

*(The "*BOY*" goes through the motions, opening the door.)*

P: Oh, sure. Yes.

*(The "*BOY*" closes the door.)*

FELLOW TRAVELER: *Tree eelee chehtyryeh?*... Three or four?

P: *(Confused)* Ah...four?

FELLOW TRAVELER: But of course, there's your family.

P: *(Quickly)* But they're not traveling with me.

FELLOW TRAVELER: Where?

P: *(Evasively)* Where I'm going.

FELLOW TRAVELER: But you're here! How many?

P: Four. With the elevator boy.

FELLOW TRAVELER: Ah! He is in your family!

P: *(Exasperated)* No! Here.

"BOY": Ding!

FELLOW TRAVELER: And here we are!

(The "BOY" opens the door. As P exits, a group of diplomats and military crowd around him. The music becomes a cocktail piano waltz.)

Scene Three: The War Room

FIELD MARSHAL: Ladies and gentlemen! Our Distinguished Guest has just arrived! Here, have some champagne.

(Drinks are served around from a tray. P doesn't quite know what's happening, but it seems less dangerous than the elevator.)

DIPLOMAT: What kept you so long?

P: What do you mean?

DIPLOMAT: What do *you* mean?

FIELD MARSHAL: Here, come this way...

GENERAL: Gentlemen! Port and cigars in the War Room. Lord Kitchener will speak to us presently.

FIELD MARSHAL: Hurry along, now!

AMBASSADOR: You've kept us waiting for hours.

P: Oh, I'm sorry. I didn't realize...

(The GENERAL takes the podium.)

GENERAL: Gentlemen, gentlemen, please!

(The small crowd quiets down and assembles before the podium.)

GENERAL: In these troubled times, besieged as we are on all fronts...

DIPLOMAT: Here! Here!

GENERAL: There is but one man in whom we can place with complete assurance our Faith, Hope and Destiny...

FIELD MARSHAL: There! There!

GENERAL: A man who has won more battles than he has fought!

AMBASSADOR: Where? Where?

GENERAL: A man who has the confidence of his people! Our generated, veneered leader! Our own Fighting Jack! Lord Kerchner...er, Kitchener!

(The crowd applauds wildly. The ancient Lord KITCHENER, using a walker, toddles out to the podium. He clutches it. He silences the crowd with a gesture, coughs discreetly, clears his throat and is about to speak when he coughs again. The GENERAL hands him a glass of water. Lord KITCHENER takes a long swallow and begins a coughing spasm. He drops the water glass. The fit becomes worse and worse until KITCHENER, red-faced, strangles and falls to the floor. There is a brief pause, then the group begins applauding and murmuring quiet approval. P is appalled by what he's witnessed. He goes to the podium and appeals to the crowd.)

P: But... He's...he's dead!

(An obvious revolutionary girl, "PATTI," armed to the teeth, rushes in, give KITCHENER a poke with the end of her automatic weapon, threatens the crowd, which quickly disperses, and holds her weapon on P.)

PATTI: You'd better come with us.

P: I... I can't...

PATTI: We're no longer safe here. We must go to the Winter Palace, quickly!

(PATTI *hustles* P *off stage and out.*)

Scene Four: The Winter Palace

(*An arena in which many revolutionary activities could take place. A musical fanfare. The* RINGLEADER *gets hit by a spot.*)

RINGLEADER: (*Speaking in a heavy accent*) Und yetz! Pear-formingk LIVE from here—Ze Greadt Doomed Ice Pallast mitten ouren Happy Gnackvurts Brooders, Hans undt Yoni! Ze New Puppet Government!!

(*Huge recorded applause. Music plays.* P *and* PATTI *return as the show begins.* PATTI *keeps a wary eye out for trouble. Whatever the "Show" is in this particular production, [Acrobatic Garden Gnomes? Killer Klowns on Skates? Hand Puppet Government?] the Brothers begin their act with great bravado.*)

YONI: Hello! Hello!

HANS: Hello! Hello!

YONI: Say Hello Hans!

HANS: Hello Hans!

YONI: No, you dumbelly!

(HANS *give a punch to* YONI. *Recorded laughter.* HANS *pulls out a gun and shoots at* HANS. *The crowd laughs again.* YONI *pulls out a gun and shoots at* HANS. *More laughter.* HANS *mimes lobbing a hand-grenade at* YONI. YONI *mimes a rocket launcher. Screams of laughter. There's a really big explosion. The air is suddenly filled with rockets and bomb blasts. Screams, not laughter from the crowd. An air-raid siren sounds, lights flash red.* HANS *and* YONI, *both badly wounded, are now firing into the crowd. P ducks out of the way, but* PATTI *is hit and drops dramatically dead.)*

(A big revolutionary, PANCHO VILLA, *makes his way to* P *without getting hit and crouches down beside him.)*

PANCHO: Psssst! Which side are you on?

P: Which side? Side two.

PANCHO: Then you're with us! Come with me!

*(*PANCHO *pushes* P *ahead of him, away from the violence now fading as* HANS *and* YONI's *puppet government falls.)*

P: Where are you taking me?

(P and PANCHO *walk briskly in place, as though down a long corridor, their footsteps echoing.)*

Scene Five: The Protocol

(The two are joined progressively by four more revolutionaries until there is quite a little band, all walking rapidly in place. The speeches are delivered with great intensity, sotto voce, overlapping.)

*(*TRENCHCOAT MAN *is the first to join the cadre.)*

PANCHO: We don't have much time...

TRENCHCOAT MAN: ...and there's a lot you have to know.

*(*MAOGIRL *catches up, and then* CHE.)*

MAOGIRL: Please listen carefully. If the Revolution is to be successful...

CHE: Excuse me. Wait. Wait...

TRENCHCOAT MAN: No, look, first...

MAOGIRL: But... no, no...

PANCHO: But, but...

CHE: This is important! The Revolutionary Leadership...

MAOGIRL: No, listen! I'm talking about the Codification...

TRENCHCOAT MAN: Go ahead, go ahead...

CHE: The Codification is...

PANCHO: The Codification is the Central Control...

CHE: Wait, wait, wait, wait!

MAOGIRL: No, no, no, no...

(An ARAB YOUTH *joins them.)*

ARAB YOUTH: This is Top Secret...

PANCHO: Top Secret...

TRENCHCOAT MAN: Top Secret

ARAB YOUTH & CHE: Excuse me! The Protocol! The Protocol!

MAOGIRL: Don't tell him about the situation yet!

TRENCHCOAT MAN: No. Let me! Let me...do you mind?

PANCHO: But the Codification...

ARAB YOUTH: The Central Control...

TRENCHCOAT MAN: Don't forget the Protocol...

MAOGIRL: No, please! Do you mind?

CHE: All right, go ahead.

PANCHO & TRENCHCOAT MAN: Go ahead.

CHE & MAOGIRL: Go ahead. Go ahead.

ARAB YOUTH: I was only going to...

MAOGIRL & TRENCHCOAT MAN: The expediency, the expediency...

ARAB YOUTH: According to regulations...

(P has been listening intently to the gabble. At the word "Regulations," he makes a decision to take control.)

P: Check!

ARAB YOUTH & TRENCHCOAT MAN: Right!

CHE & PANCHO: Right!

MAOGIRL: Everything has got to be done in this time...

ALL FIVE REVOLTIONARIES: We've got to have Priority of Rank...

P: Right!

MAOGIRL: Do you mind if I...

PANCHO: Go!

ARAB YOUTH: Go right ahead.

MAOGIRL: There is Absolute Security necessitated...

TRENCHCOAT MAN: No, no, no...

P: Right! Check!

MAOGIRL: ...in all of these Operations...

TRENCHCOAT MAN: But, but, but...

PANCHO: No, no, no...

ARAB YOUTH: Go on, go on, go on...

CHE: Let me, let me, let me...

P: *(He stops walking)* I'll take it from here. Follow me!

(The five REVOLUTIONARIES stop walking and give P a brisk salute.)

REVOLUTIONARIES: Right, Chief!

Scene Six: The Speech

(We are in the Great Hall of the People. The
REVOLUTIONARIES *quickly become Security Guards, audibly
"checking" the doors, aisles and audience members. P makes
his way to the podium, shaking hands, murmuring words to
patrons, much as the President does when making the State
of the Union speech. Modestly, he quiets the audience. His
voice booms and echoes from the speakers.)*

P: Gentlemen! Ladies! Thank you...I won't take any
more credit for this Victory than is necessary. Lord
Kitchener did not—hell, *will not*—die in vain, Grid
willing! ... *(Modestly acknowledging the audience's
response)* Thank you... No...I as Leader will use Power
like a drum and Leadership like a violin. Pick out
any Idea. Compare Ideas. With the One Idea left,
you have no Doubt, and without a Doubt, we have
Enthusiasm!...

(The REVOLUTIONARIES *salute their Leader and cry out
foreign-sounding words:)*

REVOLUTIONARIES: Prego! Prego! Pardon! Pardon!
Shoes For Industry! Viva el maximo lee-dair!

P: Please...thank you so very much...yes... To make Life
hold...it's as easy as a Bridge! Yes, now! Now, ladies
and gentlemen, now that we have attained Control, we
must pull together as One. Like a Twin! Keeping the
Prophecy of Power as Enthusiasm! All for One!

REVOLUTIONARIES: All for One!

P: And All for One!

REVOLUTIONARIES: And All for One!!

P: *(He's got them in the palm of his hand now:)* Let Me
hear it for Me!

REVOLUTIONARIES: *(No, they've got him—in the sights of
their weapons)* You're under arrest!

(The lights go out.)

Scene Seven: The Prison

(A great prison door clangs shut. One dim light shines on a Sexy Woman PRISONER, *sitting on a cot, reading an old pulp magazine with a lurid cover. [All the other* PRISONERS *in this scene are "off stage."]* P, *much the worse for wear, stumbles out of the darkness and collapses at the foot of the cot.)*

SEXY PRISONER: Hello! My, it will be pleasant to have you here. I haven't had any company in this dank and dismal cell for many long and miserable years... *(She reads from the magazine.)* "I was imprisoned by a faceless people for a crime of which I had no knowledge and certainly did not commit. But what of that? In my spare time I have been pursuing my hobby, which is to write a Great Prison Novel. In the beginning, I wrote with an ink composed of parts of my own blood. However, this would not make an acceptable copy, so I acquired an electric typewriter." *(To* P, *pulling him up onto the cot)* I am proud to present you with the first edition of my saga of eternal torment—profusely illustrated—titled "Leather Thighs."

*(*SEXY PRISONER *hands* P *the magazine.* P *looks at it, looks at the Prisoner, writhing sexily, and screams:)*

P: Guard! Guard! I want to see my Ambassador!

ARAB PRISONER: *(Laughing)* That is easily done! He is in the next cell!

LATINO PRISONER: You can use the telephone!

P: But—I don't have a dime.

SEXY PRISONER: You could use one of the pages of my dime novel.

(Not surprisingly, there is an old-fashioned phone on the floor under the bed. P grabs the phone and sits on the cot next to the recumbent SEXY PRISONER. *P dials and waits. All we can hear are the tapping footsteps of Fred Astaire.)*

P: It's no good. They're tapping the lines... Oh, if I could only speak to someone...

(The SEXY *PRISIONER stretches out alluringly, as if to say "How about me?")*

P: If only I could tell my story!

(The SEXY PRISONER *leans up to wrap her arms around* P *when two figures appear—the* BIG SCREW *and the* FAMOUS WRITER.*)*

SCREW: Famous Writer to see the condemned man!

("Condemned man?!" P *leaps from the cot.)*

FAMOUS WRITER: *(Turned way on)* Oh...you poor brute of a killer without a conscience! I'm wet with compassion!

P: No! I'm not a killer...

(The SEXY PRISONER *rises sexily and undulates toward the* FAMOUS WRITER, *her hand out.)*

SEXY PRISONER: Excuse me, but it's always a pleasure to meet another member of the writing fraternity. Maybe you'd like to hear a chapter from my Great Prison Novel of Eternal Torment... "In Cold Leather"...

*(*SEXY PRISONER *plucks the magazine from* P's *hand and goes off arm-in-arm with the* FAMOUS WRITER. P *slumps in despair on the cot.)*

P: Oh, God...

(In a nimbus of light, God, in the person of Pat O'Brien, speaks through the big speakers.)

GOD: Aye, what's troublin' ye, son?

P: Padre... I'm tired of living and... and...

SINGING PRISONER: "Feared of dyin'...that Old Man River, he just...

HECKLING PRISONER: Ribbah! Ribbah! Old Man Ribbah!!

SINGING PRISONER: *(Awkwardly)* Ribb-ah... Ribbah...

GOD: Now, son, give me your gun.

P: But, I don't have a gun, Father.

GOD: Well, then, you can have one of mine!

(GOD tosses P a pistol. P looks at it, calculates the chances of escape, realizes it's hopeless and tosses the pistol on the cot. From all around come the cat-calls of the other PRISONERS.)

PRISONERS: Ya! Ya! Chicken! Fraidy-cat! Wimp! Four-eyes! Nerd! Yellow-belly! Deserter! Terrorist!

P: No, look, everybody! I'm not afraid of Justice! I know these bars are here for a good reason! Prisons are for the guilty!

ARAB PRISONER: String him up!

HECKLING PRISONER: Anybody got any string?

LATINO PRISONER: He looks just like The Kid!

P: No, no, no! Don't you guys see? The System is here for your protection! I'm not afraid! All I want is a chance to clear my name! Look, we live and operate under due process of Law. The Innocent have nothing to fear! Only the Guilty will suffer!

ARAB PRISONER: Lynch him!

HECKLING PRISONER: Anybody got any lynch?

LATINO PRISONER: He even looks like The Kid!

P: Look! Look! It's this simple! I'll get a hearing and a trial. I'm willing to place my Fate and Faith in the Hands of Justice!

(The lights dim, there is a loud electrical zzzappp and a volley of rifle shots. A scream off-stage.)

P: What... What happened to the lights?

PRISONERS: They just burned The Kid...

P: *(He realizes justice isn't so easy to come by as the imagined. Panic sets in.)* Mamma! Mamma! I'll be good, Mamma! I will, Mamma. I'll be good, Mamma! I just want to get out!! *(He collapses on the cot, stretched out, covered in sweat.)*

Scene Eight: Beat The Reaper

(P moans in fever and pain. The lights begin to twirl and blaze. A suspense chord of music sustains as JUDY *and* DR FILTH *both gaze at poor, sick* P.)

JUDY: Do you think he's going to make it, Doctor Filth?

DR FILTH: I don't know, Judy. He looks pretty sick to me.

P: *(Groaning)* What happened? Where am I?

JUDY: Wow! Listen! I think he's coming around... !

DR FILTH: *(Chiming in)* You're right! He's coming around!

(Suddenly, into the spotlight steps the Star of the Show JERRY YARROW! *This is T V hottest new reality quiz.)*

JERRY: Heeee's coming around, folks! He's going to be O K and ready to play Symptom Six of "Beat The Reaper!"

(The theme music kicks in and we are on the set. The show continually pumps up anxiety, adrenalin, dread and greed.)

JUDY: Last week our Patient successfully survived the common cold, measles, pneumonia, dengue fever and the yaws...

JERRY: And now—The Big Question! Are you ready to Go On?

(Leaning over P's writhing body, JERRY holds the mike up to P's lips. We can hardly hear him.)

P: What's... yaws... ?

JERRY: He's ready!

JUDY: I just can't believe it!

DR FILTH: Seal our Patient back into the Isolation Ward, please!

(Suspense music as DR FILTH takes out a big hypodermic.)

JERRY: Can you hear me in there, patient?

P: No...

JERRY: O K! Let's shoot him up!

(DR FILTH *brutally injects about a quart of vile disease into* P.)

JERRY: Now, Patient, you have ten seconds to tell us what you've got and "Beat The Reaper!"

(A clock theme counts down the time. P quickly reports his symptoms.)

P: Ah...I'm shaky...I'm feverish...my hands are all...I'm turning yellow! ...My God! I've got jaundice!

(Happy music)

JUDY: Jaundice is right! Please, give him the antidote, Doctor!

(DR FILTH *wipes the hypo off and squirts another dose into* P's *other arm. Cheers from the crowd)*

JERRY: Well, folks, that's symptom Six! And now our patient has reached the Final Threshold on "Beat The Reaper!" Here's the Question, kid... Are you ready for Symptom Number Seven?

JUDY: That's longer than any Patient has ever survived before!

P: I don't think so... I want to go home...

JERRY: Only one way to do that! Doctor, bring in the Super Shot!

JUDY: For the first time on "Beat The Reaper!" we're going for the Big Disease! The icebox is being unlocked by the President of the Armenian Medical Association, under whose strict supervision these toxins are being administered.

(DR FILTH *has a portable ice chest, of the sort that might hold a donated organ in dry ice. He unlocks the chest and it opens with a blast of steam. He takes out a small vial, which he opens, carries over to P and empties on his outstretched arm. We can't see what it is. The* DR FILTH *peers at the arm with a magnifying glass. He winces, then nods at* JERRY.)

JERRY: Now, Patient, you've got just ten seconds to tell us what you've got and, for the very last time, "Beat The Reaper!"

(The clock ticks.)

P: I feel... (Coughing) ...I think I feel...I don't know... whatever it is... I want to die...

(The clock runs out. A great honking "Wrong!" buzzer sounds. Game's over. JUDY shrieks with disappointment.)

JERRY: Oh, I'm terribly sorry, that's not correct! You didn't "Beat The Reaper!" Doctor, let's bring the Patient out and show the amphitheatre audience and all the folks at home just what he's contracted.

(The ATTENDANTS *bring* P *out.* DR FILTH *takes his pulse, looks in his eyes, examines the flea bite on his arm and presents the empty vial to* JERRY.)

DR FILTH: According to my careful prosthesis, this man has the Plague.

JERRY: Thank you, Doctor.

DR FILTH: You're welcome.

JUDY: Wow! You've got the Plague!

P: Plague? I never would've guessed you'd give me the Plague!

JERRY: Isn't he a good sport, folks!

P: What's the antidote? Hey!

(P appeals to the DR FILTH who shrugs, looks at his watch and leaves. JERRY turns to face another Camera as commercial T V life goes on.)

JERRY: We'll be back in just a moment with our next patient, but first this word for Greed!...

(Music theme plays out as the action continues.)

Scene Nine: The Taxi

(Everyone is abuzz with "plague". The word travels around the room. At first, people try to break through the "walls" of the Isolation Ward. Then P runs. He runs, pursued by plague-seeking people, as if he were saving his own life, rather than theirs. As he is almost ready to stop and let whatever might happen go ahead and happen, a taxicab pulls up beside him and the TAXI DRIVER gestures for him to get in. The TAXI DRIVER is the woman who has been watching him from the beginning.)

TAXI DIVER: Taxi, buddy?

P: Oh, thank God!

TAXI DIVER: Not yet. Where to, kid?

P: Out! Out of the country!

TAXI DIVER: Sure thing!

(The TAXI DRIVER *puts the taxi in gear and they roar off, chase music building behind them.)*

TAXI DIVER: I'll take you right to the Border. We're gonna have to cut through the Park, though.

P: Is that the fastest way?

TAXI DIVER: Well, no, it's not, but the Plague's got the streets all tied up

(The taxi speeds up.)

P: Please! As fast as you can!

TAXI DIVER: I'm doin' my best!

(P relaxes a moment, spots something, then looks under his seat and pulls out his backpack. The Mickey Mouse bag comes out with it.)

P: Hey! Wait a minute! Is this my bag?

TAXI DIVER: Sure is, kid!

(P realizes that this woman is the same one he's seen all along.)

P: You're the same one...you were even in the prison!

TAXI DIVER: Check! We've been watchin' you every step of the way, but we haven't had a chance to contact you 'til now.

P: You mean...? You mean...?

TAXI DIVER: Listen, honey, let me give you a piece of advice. What you don't mean won't hurt you.

P: But I didn't mean...

TAXI DIVER: Mind if I turn on the News?

P: Whatever...

(The TAXI DRIVER *punches a remote which causes us to see the* ANCHORMAN *in the Studio in the midst of his spiel.)*

ANCHORMAN: *(Ed)* ...in a massive traffic tie-up, as the death-rate continues to soar. Now, let's go down to the river's edge, and Charles B Smith...

(Smith, an elderly network pundit, is doing a stand-up in front of the river. All the action he describes is happening behind him as he looks at us through the camera eye.)

SMITH: Ed, it's an amazing scene here. Like lemmings, the crowds are waiting on the shore, torches blazing, as the long line of shrouded funeral rafts drift lazily into view... *(Glancing back at them)* ...great black candles flickering at helm and stern. The excitement is contagious and so are the Black Cross Volunteers as they pass from family to family, pausing now and again to touch a child's head. *(He looks sadly back once more)* I wish I could...but I can't...so long, Ed...

(We see the ANCHORMAN again. P leans forward and looks for the remote control.)

ANCHORMAN: *(Ed)* Thank you, Charles. And now, here's another feature in our continuing report on the...

(P finds the remote and clicks the ANCHORMAN off.)

P: How close are we to the Border?

TAXI DIVER: Well, at this rate, I don't...oh, oh! I think they've spotted you!

(The taxi "drives" into a crowd of PLAGUE-SEEKERS, all of them screaming and grabbing at the car and P.)

PLAGUE-SEEKERS: I want to die! There he is! He's got it! Me! Me! Give it to me! What about me?

TAXI DIVER: *(Leaning out to yell at the crowd blocking his way)* Get out of the way! Go find your own carrier! I've got mine!

P: Can't we go any faster?

TAXI DIVER: There's too many of them.

P: What can we do?

TAXI DIVER: I don't know... Maybe—throw them your jacket.

(P takes off his jacket and cautiously tosses it out to the crowd. A person snatches it and runs.)

PLAGUE-SEEKERS: Me! Me! Throw it to me! I want to die!

TAXI DIVER: There's the Border up ahead!

P: Thank God!

TAXI DIVER: I told you—not yet! We'll never make it through that crowd at the Gate unless you do exactly what I say. Take off your clothes!

P: What?

TAXI DIVER: Come on, honey! Take 'em off!

P: All right...

(P takes off his shirt and pants, then his socks, as the TAXI DRIVER careens through the slow-motion crowd of plague-seekers hurling themselves at the taxi. P considers his boxers and decides against it.)

P: That's everything...

TAXI DIVER: O K. When I give the signal, toss them out and I'll drive this heap right through the barrier. Ready? Here we go!

PLAGUE-SEEKERS: Me! Me! Me!

TAXI DIVER: Now!

(P opens the taxi door and flings the garments out to the crowd that fights for them and runs off rubbing them all over their plague-ridden bodies. They fall behind as the taxi crashes through the barrier with a loud skid and reverberating crash. There is no light.)

Scene 10: The Border

(Out of the darkness and silence we hear P running, panting with exhaustion. He staggers into the light, breathing deeply. A VOICE *is heard over the speakers.)*

VOICE: Hurry... Over here... This way... That's it! You've made it. Welcome to Side Six.

P: *(Murmuring)* Side... Six... ?

VOICE: Follow in your book and repeat after me as we learn our next three words in Turkish... Coffee...

P: Wait a second... wait! Coff-ee...

VOICE: Dee-light!

P: Dee-light...

VOICE: Bor-der...

P: Bor-der... No! Wait!

(P realizes he must go through everything once more and tries to run away in slow motion as the VOICE *slows down like a faulty old record.)*

VOICE: May...I...seeeee...yourrrrr...pass...port...pleeee-se...

(The lights slowly fade out as P continues running nowhere.)

END OF PLAY

ADAPTOR'S NOTE

ELECTRICIAN, as I first produced it, required only an army cot and a velvet rope between two chromium stands as stage furniture. More important were the two large "Big Brother" speakers on either side of the playing area.

We did the show with an ensemble cast of ten, including the young actor (my son Orson) playing "P" and the only woman, who appears in disguise in each of the ten scenes.

The piece opens with P's existential arrival at the Border. Here the surreal nightmare begins. Borders have not changed much in the years since "Electrician" was written. Entrenched governments continue to prop themselves up. Revolutions continue to create "puppet governments." Writers are still thrown into dungeons. And the plague? It's always a hot commodity, and folks will kill themselves to get it.

But, again and again, we all approach the Borders in our lives, never knowing what we will find, or what might find us, on the Other Side. Transitions are the hardest part.

A few suggestions: Have as much fun as you can with the props and costumes, since the stage is largely bare. Contemporize any of the characters to fit your whims or the Evening News.

The "Fellow Traveler" in Scene 2 speaks both Russian and French as glibly as possible.

Scene 4—The Winter Palace is open for any sort of specialty act your production might have or, simply, a pair of hand-puppets.

In the Prison, Scene 7, the "Sexy Prisoner" is straight out of an exploitation movie and wears leather.

David Ossman

TEMPORARILY
HUMBOLDT COUNTY
or,
Manifest Destiny,
Take 2

(The scene: Against a backdrop of the prairies, two INDIANS *in full warrior costume and makeup watch as a herd of buffalo pass slowly by.)*

INDIAN: Well, I think it's about time. The way the corn's been growing for the last two generations...

SECOND INDIAN: Look at that herd of buffalo! They're ready!

INDIAN: Everything's living the Great Spirit's Way—in Harmony.

SECOND INDIAN: He'll be here soon.

INDIAN: The True While Brother is coming home. Remember what the Great Spirit said? If we did what we were supposed to do, and lived according to the Plan, White Brother would finish his work in the East and come back to us.

SECOND INDIAN: It'll be nice to have the Family together again!

(A CONQUISTADOR, *a* PADRE *and several* SPANISH SOLDIERS *enter to a trumpet fanfare and flamenco music. The buffalo scatter.)*

CONQUISTADOR: *Buenos dias, amigos!*

INDIAN: Hello! You must be the True White Brother!

CONQUISTADOR: Sure! You must be the Indians!

INDIAN: Yes!

SECOND INDIAN: Welcome home!

(All the SPANISH SOLDIERS *cheer.)*

CONQUISTADOR: Welcome to New Spain! This is your new Father—Father Corona.

FATHER CORONA: *(He's Irish!)* Pax venuti nictum! Down on your knees, now! D'ye recognize what I'm holdin' over your heads, lads?

INDIAN: It's a Cross. The Symbol of the Quartering of the Universe into Active and Passive Principles.

FATHER CORONA: God have mercy on their heathen souls!

CONQUISTADOR: What the Father means is—what is the Cross made of? Gold! Have you got any?

INDIAN: No...

CONQUISTADOR: What about the Seven Cities of Gold? Phoenix? Tucson? Las Vegas?

SECOND INDIAN: This is gold.

CONQUISTADOR: What's that?

INDIAN: Corn.

SPANISH SOLDIER: Corn! Now we can make tortillas!

SECOND SPANISH SOLDIER: We've been waiting for this for hundreds of years!

THIRD SPANISH SOLDIER: I just invented tacos!

CONQUISTADOR: So, is this all you've got?

INDIAN: Yes...but aren't you the True White Brother who's supposed to come and live with us in peace?

CONQUISTADOR: Sure! Therefore, I claim this rich, verdant pasture land in the name of the Empire of Spain!

VESPUCCI: *(He's Italian!)* Hey! Hey, Capitano! The rain, she's a-stoppa to fall! And the corn, she's all dead!

CONQUISTADOR: Shudduppa' Vespucch'! I claim this stinking desert in the name of the Empire of Spain. Forever! Let's go!

(The SPANISH SOLDIERS *grumble. The buffalo herd mills about.)*

SPANISH SOLDIERS: *(Singing)* God bless Vespucciland, mmm-mmm-mmm...

FATHER CORONA: Oh, by the way, Domini Domini Domini! You're all Catholics now! God bless you!

CONQUISTADOR: Come on, Father. No one in their right mind would live in this stinking desert.

THIRD SPANISH SOLDIER: Come on, Cisco!

(The Spaniards leave and the Indians hide as a wagon train enters. One PIONEER *plays* Oh, Susanna *on his harmonica.* ANOTHER PIONEER *speaks:)*

ANOTHER PIONEER: Boy! I'm tired o' pushin' West. How long ago'd we leave Goshen?

THIRD PIONEER: 'Bout two hours ago! Ain't we ever gonna stop?

PIONEER: Quiet down now, boys. Wagon Boss is gonna speak!

WAGON BOSS: My fellow settlers! We stand her at the Edge O' Civilization, on the banks of the Mississsouri River, lookin' West, at Our Destiny!

PIONEER: You can say that again!

WAGON BOSS: What may appear to the faint-hearted as a limitless expanse of Godforsaken wilderness...

THIRD PIONEER: Sure is!

WAGON BOSS: ...is, in reality, a Golden Opportunity for humble, God-fearin' people like ourselves, an' our families, an' our children, an' the generations a-comin', to carve a new life—outta the American Indian!

(The INDIANS *come out of hiding.)*

INDIAN: Welcome, White Brother!

WAGON BOSS: Injuns! Draw the wagons up into a circle!

INDIAN: Why do you always do that?

WAGON BOSS: We git better reception that-a way. Mind if I put this antenna up on yonder peak?

SECOND INDIAN: That's our Sacred Mountain.

WAGON BOSS: This is our Sacred Antenna! It's shaped like a cross. Made out of aluminum. Er—got any aluminum?

INDIAN: We've still got some corn left.

PIONEER: Hey! Corn! Now we can make whisky!

ANOTHER PIONEER: We've been waitin' hundreds o' years fer this!

THIRD PIONEER: Say! I just invented a Tom Collins!

WAGON BOSS: Here, Injun. Ya want some firewater?

INDIAN: No. We were warned by our Elders not to drink anything that would make us weak or silly.

WAGON BOSS: *(Laughs)* Put it in their well.

SECOND INDIAN: That's not a well. It's the eye of the Holy Serpent Mound, on which you're standing.

WAGON BOSS: It's a beaut'!

INDIAN: No, it's a mound.

WAGON BOSS: And right purty, too! Er—can ya move it?

INDIAN: But, why?

WAGON BOSS: Railroad's comin' though! Right now!

(A railroad train loaded with COWBOYS *and* RAILROADERS *pulls in. The buffalo are scattered and the herd is split.)*

COWBOY: Hey! What're we stoppin' fer?

RAILROADER: Are we in Goshen yet?

CONDUCTOR: Cain't go no further. This here's Injun Territory!

GOVERNMENT AGENT: Well, then! It's Treaty Time!

(Brass Band enters, playing Hail To The Chief.*)*

GOVERNMENT AGENT: My fellow Redskins! Speaking for the Great White Father in Washington and all the American People, let me say we respect you savages for your Native Ability to instantly Adapt and Survive in whatever Godforsaken wilderness we move you to. Out there. Sign here!

(The INDIANS *shrug and put "X"s on the paper.)*

RAILROADER: They did it!

(All the COWBOYS *whoop and holler. The train and brass band leave.)*

INDIAN: No reason to complain. It's not so bad out there. We still have our People and our Ceremonies and the Sun, Moon and Stars, and the Sand, and the Black Stuff coming out of the ground...

GOVERNMENT AGENT: Black Stuff comin' out of the ground?

TRAILBLAZER: Civilization, ho-oooooo!

(A passel of Sooners, dogs, Model Ts and dust storms passes by, leaving the INDIANS *alone. The wind blows.)*

SECOND INDIAN: It's nice out here in the desert. No rain, no crops, no White Brother.

(A Greyhound tour bus pulls up, stops and the passengers file out.)

BUS DRIVER: All out for Fort Stinkin' Desert! Last Indian Reservation for two thousand miles. You got fifteen minutes, folks. Get 'em while you can!

(Several shots ring out.)

BUS DRIVER: Get the Senator back in the bus!

(The SENATOR fires off more shots at the INDIANS as he is led away.)

SENATOR: Godfrey Daniel! Pesky Redskins! Which way's Goshen?

TOURIST: Howdy, there, Colorful Replicas of America's Past! When is the exciting-in-its-primitive-splendor Snake Dance going to take place?

INDIAN: It's usually in August, but with our children off in Indian School, there's no one left to do the ceremonies.

(EDDIE gets off the bus.)

EDDIE: Hiya, Pop! I'm home!

SECOND INDIAN: Hello, Soaring Eagle! It's good to have you back from school!

EDDIE: Aw, come on! Call me Eddie. I'm an American now!

SECOND INDIAN: What have they been teaching you?

EDDIE: Just what we need for a better life! French horn, Italian, water polo...

GOVERNMENT AGENT: Yes, at Custer Memorial Indian School, Eddie's one of our Prize Students. We're giving him away next week.

INDIAN: Oh, my White Brother.

(A hippie FREAK gets off the bus.)

FREAK: Hey, man! Don't let him bring you down, now. There's a lot of young people in this country, just like myself, who really know where the Indian's at. And don't worry. Soon we're all gonna be out here on the Reservation, livin' like Indians, 'n' dressin' like Indians and doin' all the simple, beautiful things that you Indians do. Hey—got any peyote?

RICH TOURIST: Say, how much is that necklace you're wearing?

LADY TOURIST: Does anybody here know how to do the War Dance?

TOURIST WITH CAMERA: Hold it! Smile!

RICH TOURIST: Isn't it amazing how they survive on this stinking desert?

LAUGHING TOURIST: Ya got any scalps?

TOURIST WITH CAMERA: Lemme get a shot of you and yer squaw.

RICH TOURIST: Let's see the War Dance!

LADY TOURIST: Let's see you dance!

TOURISTS: Let's see the Dance! Dance! Dance! Dance! Dance!

(More shots ring out. The Indians dance in a circle.

BUS DRIVER: O K! O K, folks! Fun's over! Back on the bus!

MOTHER: Where's little Billy Joe?

FATHER: He's in that run-down outhouse over there, Mamma.

INDIAN: That's our Sun Altar.

GOVERNMENT AGENT: Well, Injuns, just goes to show you there's an obvious need to conserve our Priceless National Heritage. The Government is turning your home into a National Monument!

(The marching band gets off the bus, playing America The Beautiful. *The* SENATOR *follows.)*

SENATOR: It behooves me, 'pon this Historic Occasion, to dedicate the Stinkin' Desert National Historical Monument and Cobalt Testing Range!

TRAILBLAZER: Civilization, ho-ooooooo!

(As the INDIANS *watch, the cobalt bomb goes off. The sound dies away after a time, and the smoke clears, revealing the two* INDIANS *back on horseback.)*

INDIAN: Well, it's about time. There's been no corn growing for the last few generations. The buffalo's gone. There's no one left to live in harmony.

SECOND INDIAN: I wonder where we went wrong?

INDIAN: Let's just keep to the Life Plan. Remember what the Great White Spirit said: "Follow the Peaceful Way." The True White Brother is bound to come.

(An ASSISTANT MOVIE DIRECTOR *runs on, yelling through a megaphone.)*

ASSISTANT DIRECTOR: All right, Indians! Get ready!

(A SECOND ASSISTANT *follows, with a clap-stick.)*

SECOND ASSISTANT: *Winning Of The West—The Massacre.* Take four! *(He claps the clap-stick to start a take.)*

INDIAN: Well, let's go...

(SECOND ASSISTANT *and* SECOND INDIAN *join a dozen others, war-painted, who ride up beside him. Then they all gallop away in to the sunset, whooping.)*

END OF PLAY